WEAVING

CONTENTS

Curriculum Materials Center
Pope Pius XII Library
St. Joseph College
West Hartford, Ct. 06117

INTRODUCTION TO WEAVING	2
PAPER WEAVING	
Table mats	4
A FEW IDEAS	
Games boards	6
Pencil pot	7
MAKING BASKETS	8
WEAVING ON VARIOUS LOOMS	
Tangle weaving	10
Cardboard loom	11
Shoe-box loom	12
Wooden loom	13
Fringing	14
Some ideas	15
WEAVING WITHOUT A LOOM	
Wall hanging	16
Cardboard fish	17
GOD'S EYES	18
TWIG WEAVING	20
WEAVING WITH NATURAL OBJECTS	
Wall hanging	22
Flax baskets	23
WEAVE A BULLETIN BOARD	24

A Read-about

INTRODUCTION TO
WEAVING

Discovering how to weave single strands of plant or animal fibre into one solid piece was one of the human race's earliest achievements.

We can imagine one of our primitive ancestors observing a tangle of intertwined vines or grasses, studying a woven spider's web or watching a small bird weave grasses to make a basket-nest.

Whatever inspired that first early man or woman to attempt to weave, the method of weaving has remained basically the same through the ages.

Because the fibres used in weaving perish easily, none of those first woven pieces have survived. However, we do have model looms which were buried thousands of years ago in the pyramid tombs of Egyptian Pharaohs. From these, we can see that today's looms have changed very little in principle from the looms of long ago.

All weaving has two main sets of thread, the warp and the weft. (In some countries, the weft is called the woof.) The warp is the lacing thread; the weft is the filling thread. To weave, the first weft goes over/under/over the warp; the next weft, under/over/under.

In Europe a thousand years ago, large tapestries were woven by the ladies of the castles to stop draughts from blowing through the great stone halls. Many of these tapestries can still be seen in museums.

Today, woven pieces may take many forms. They may be used only for decoration or they may be important and useful items in people's daily lives.

Patterns such as these, made by plants and animals, probably inspired people's first attempts at weaving.

Did you know...

One of the most famous "weavings" of all, the 1000-year-old Bayeux Tapestry, is not woven but is a piece of embroidered linen, 70 metres (230 feet) long. The picture shows a section of this tapestry.

HOW TO DO
PAPER WEAVING

INTRODUCTION

These woven table-mats are good to make as your first weaving project — and they're useful too!

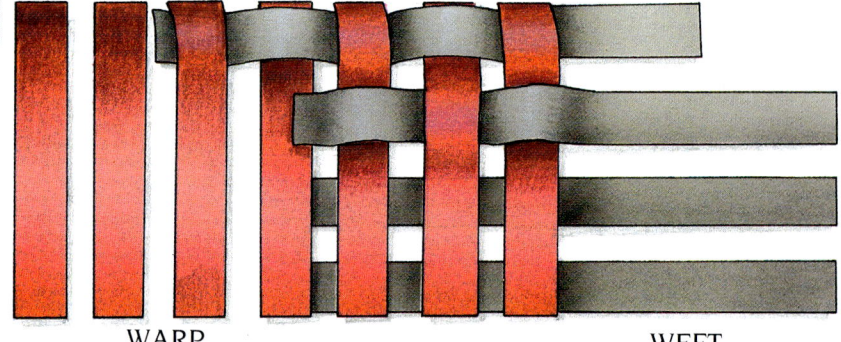

WARP　　　　　　　　WEFT

MATERIALS

2 rectangles of stiff, brightly coloured paper
Scissors
Pencil
Ruler
Transparent sticky tape

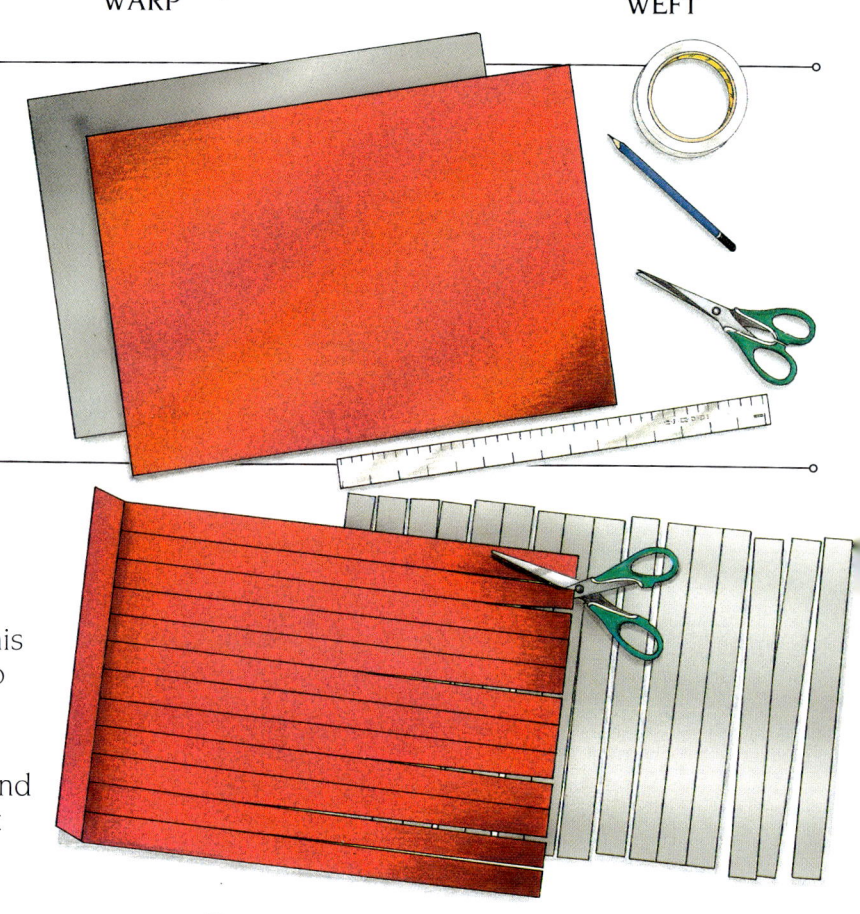

METHOD

1. Fold a ruler-wide line along a short edge of one sheet of paper.

2. Draw ruler lines up to this fold. Cut along these lines to the fold.

3. Draw ruler-wide lines across the width of the second sheet of paper. Carefully cut along these lines.

4. Start weaving: over/under/over with the first strip of weft; under/over/under with the next strip. Gently push each weft strip up against the previous one.

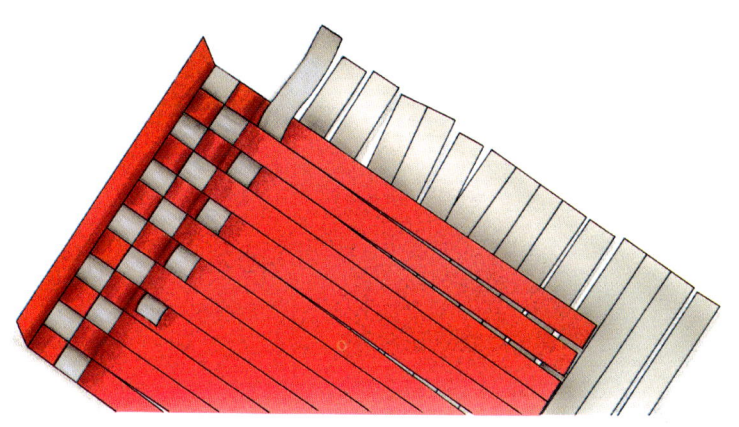

5. When all the weft strips have been woven in, turn the mat over carefully. Lay some strips of tape along the back of the weft strips to hold them in place. Cut off the strip-ends, including the first folded edge.

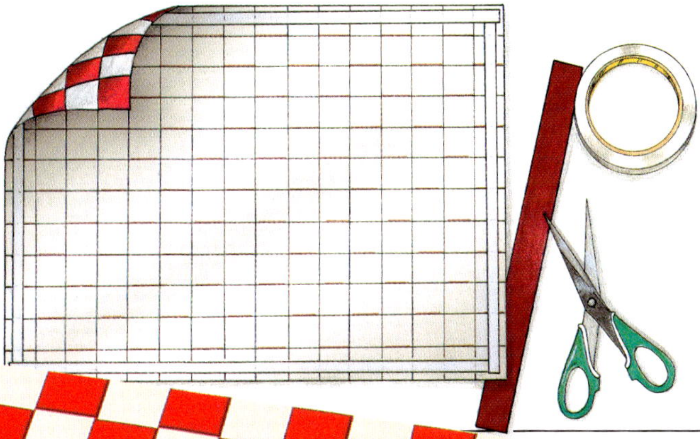

PAPER WEAVING

A FEW IDEAS

GAMES BOARDS

Try making a chess board or draughts (checkers) board.

You'll need one sheet of black paper and one of white. One sheet must be square, the other slightly rectangular to allow for the fold. It will have the same width as the first square. The length will be 3cm (1in) longer.

Begin the board in the same way as you made the table-mat, making the fold 3cm (1in) down on the larger sheet of card. A board has 64 squares, so you will cut 8 strips of warp and 8 of weft. Weave the chess board, following the table-mat directions on pages 4-5.

You could make a noughts-and-crosses (tick-tack-toe) board too. Use brightly coloured paper for this and 3 strips of warp and 3 of weft. Cut out cardboard circles and crosses for players to use.

PENCIL POT

Here's a quick and easy project that makes a useful gift.

MATERIALS

Sheets of coloured paper
Ruler
Pencil
Scissors
White glue or double-sided, transparent sticky tape
A straight-sided container

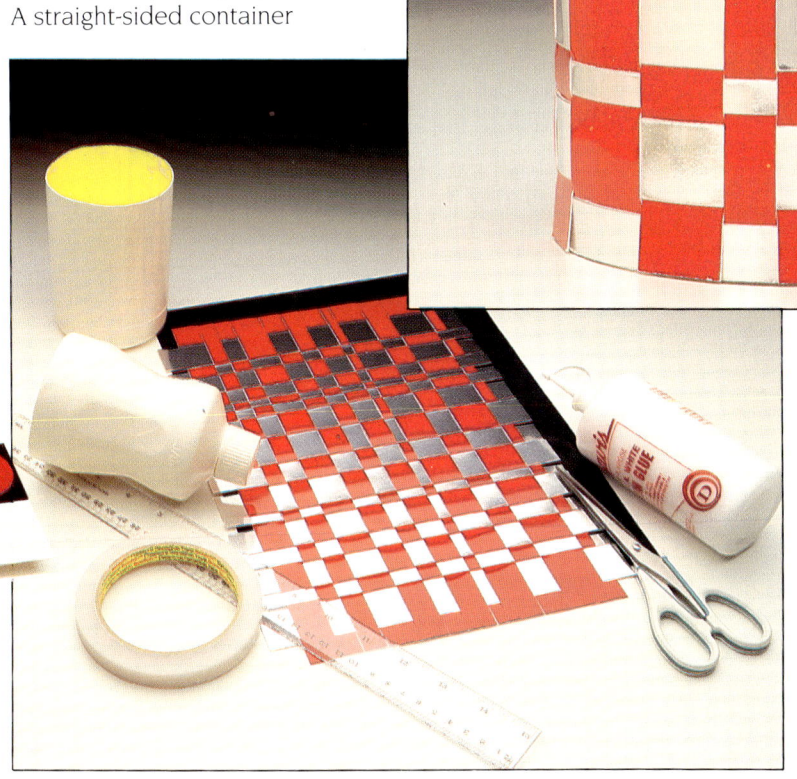

METHOD

1. Cut some wide strips of paper and some narrow ones. Use different coloured papers or foils for the weft strips.

2. Weave your mat, then use glue or tape to fasten it around the container.

Now you can fill the pot with coloured pencils.

MAKING BASKETS

SQUARE BASKETS

Fill these little baskets with small gifts.

MATERIALS

A piece of thin card for the base — a good size is 24cm square. (If you are measuring in inches, use a 12in square.)
6 strips of thin card for the weft, edge and handle — ours are 34cm long by 2cm wide (16½in by 1in).
Scissors   Pencil
Ruler   Stapler

METHOD

1. Rule the square card into nine squares. Cut off the four corner squares. Mark and cut four equal strips on each flap. Crease these flap-strips upwards.

2. Mark off four 8cm (4in) sections along four of the weft strips. (You will have a small piece left over for fastening together.) Bend each strip on the marks. Staple the ends together.

3. Gently fit one strip-square over the strip-flaps of the basket base, weaving one strip-flap under, one over, all the way round. Do the same with the next strip-square, weaving the strip-flaps in the opposite order. Do the same with the last two strip-squares. Try to end up with all the joins on the same side of the basket.

4. Fold one of the remaining long strips lengthwise and staple it round the rim of the basket to hold everything firmly and make a neat edge.

5. Staple on the last long strip for a handle.

Experiment with different numbers and sizes of warps and wefts to create different effects.

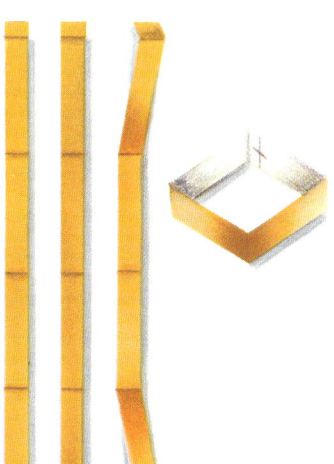
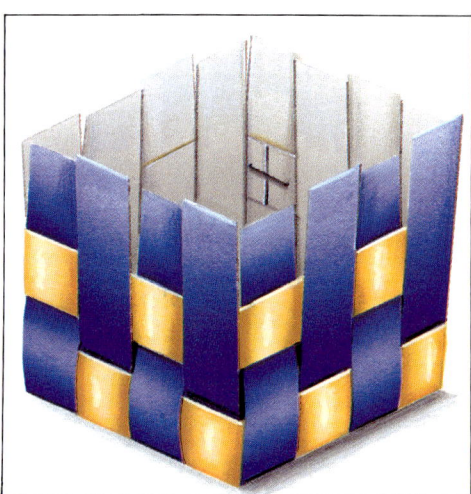

WEAVING ON
VARIOUS LOOMS

TANGLE WEAVING

If you want a wall decoration that is really interesting to look at, yet is very easy to make, try tangle weaving. One of the good things about your finished work is that no one can say, "I see a mistake!" You can't make mistakes when you weave a tangle-piece!

MATERIALS

A large piece of stiff, coloured card, plus extra strips for the frame. Our base card is 52.5cm by 45cm (20½in by 17½in). The strips are 3.5cm (1½in) wide.
Various sorts of yarns, threads or thin ribbons
Scissors
White glue or double-sided sticky tape

METHOD

1. Cut small slits anywhere around the edges of the card.

2. Slot the end of a thread into any slit, then take it over the front of the card into any other slit. This will hold the thread firmly in place. Do this with another thread, and another, until you have a crazy web all over your card. Loop a thread around a thread to change direction.

3. Now look at your card. Where threads lie fairly close together, do some over/under/over weaving. If a few threads look like wheel spokes, make a spider's web around them. Do what you like.

FRONT

BACK

4. Cut two strips of card the length of the base card, and two to match the width. Glue these border strips over the edges of the weaving, making a frame.

CARDBOARD LOOM

You can weave many different shapes on cardboard looms. A long, narrow card will make a belt; a small, square one will make a weaving that can be folded to make a glasses case. A large square will make a cushion or can be folded to make a handbag. Practise by making a glasses case.

MATERIALS

Stiff cardboard — 17cm or 7in square
Brightly coloured yarn
A large darning needle
Backing cloth (optional)

METHOD

1. Cut an even number of small slits 0.5cm (¼in) apart along two opposite edges of the card.

2. Thread a long piece of yarn back around the tabs on your card. When the card is covered, tie off the end of this yarn.

3. Thread the needle, then weave under/over/under across the top of the loom. Reverse direction and weave a second row over/under/over. Do this until the card is covered. Don't pull your weaving too tight.

4. Slip the piece of finished weaving off the card. Sew on a backing cloth, if you like. Fold in half lengthwise and bind two sides together.

WEAVING ON VARIOUS LOOMS

SHOE-BOX LOOM

The loom on which you work can be made from many different things. So far, we've looked at paper and card weaving, but now let's look at using frames.

You'll find you can do excellent woven pieces on old picture frames or on wooden frames you make for special pieces of work. A handy substitute is a shoe box.

MATERIALS

A cardboard shoe box
Yarn
Scissors
A comb or dinner fork

Shuttles cut from pieces of card — wind different coloured yarns on to these.

METHOD

1. Cut shallow slits an equal distance apart in both short ends of the box — the same number of slits at each end. Thread the warp to cover the open top of the box.

2. With yarn on a shuttle, begin to weave. Don't pull this weft too tight. Use the comb or fork to comb the woven weft threads into an evenly packed mat.

3. When your work is finished, lift it carefully off the box. Use as a small mat, or fold over to make a purse, stitching the two short sides together and adding a zipper.

If you wish, you can paint a shallow box (inside and out) in a bright colour. Weave loosely in a different colour so that the inside of the box shows through. Leave this weaving on the box. Hang it on a wall or place it on a shelf as a decoration.

WOODEN LOOM

Here's an easy way to make a loom you can use over and over again.

MATERIALS

A wooden frame, any size — 40cm by 30cm (16in by 12in) is a good size to start with
Thin nails or brads   Weaving threads
Hammer   2 thin wooden rods

METHOD

1. Hammer a row of equally spaced nails along two opposite ends of the frame. Thread the warp on to the loom. Tie off the ends.

2. This time, when you weave, don't cover the whole warp. Weave in blocks and patches of colour. However, it is a good idea to start and finish with a few lines of "right-across" weft.

3. When it's finished, gently lift the piece off the frame.

4. Carefully thread a rod through the warp loops left at the top and bottom of your woven piece. Tie a piece of string to the ends of the top rod. It is now ready to hang on the wall.

WEAVING ON VARIOUS LOOMS

FRINGING

Make a wall hanging more interesting by putting a fringe on the lower edge.

METHOD

1. Loop extra threads through the warp loops to hang down.
2. Cut the loops and knot each pair close to the lowest weft.
3. Tie beads on to these dangling threads, gather them into groups of six or so and plait (braid) them, or bind them with another piece of yarn.

It will be easier to make a fringe if you weave in a strip of card about 5cm (2in) wide before you start thread-weaving. Later, remove the card and tie the fringe close to the bottom row of weft.

SOME IDEAS

Here are some examples of woven things, some of which have been woven on a loom. Can you figure out which ones have and which haven't?

After a lot of practice you may like to try to make some of the items pictured.

WEAVING
WITHOUT A LOOM

WALL HANGING

Here's a wall hanging that doesn't need a loom or a frame! And it uses only warp threads. But there is a trick to it!

MATERIALS

A sheet of brightly coloured card
Thick yarn
Scissors
Transparent sticky tape
White glue

METHOD

1. Cut an uneven number of slits at equally spaced points along the top of the card.

2. Cut the same number of strands of yarn, the length of the card. Slot these into the slits along the top of the card and fasten behind with tape.

3. Take the outside strand of yarn from one side and weave it under/over/under the other yarns. Take the yarn at the other side of the card and weave it back beneath the first strand.

4. Continue doing this until all the lengths of yarn except the centre one have been used. You will notice that your woven piece has become narrower and narrower!

5. Put a small dab of glue behind the top ends of each weft row. Press down where glued. Leave your hanging to dry.

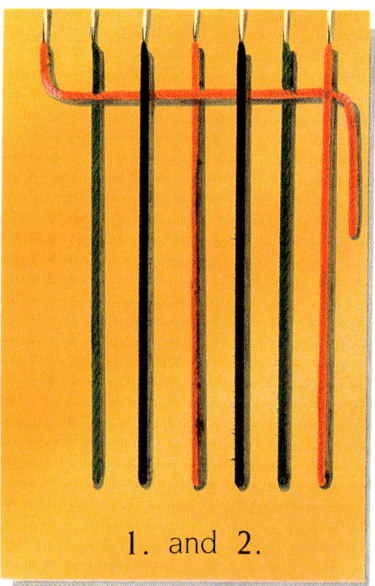
1. and 2.

3.

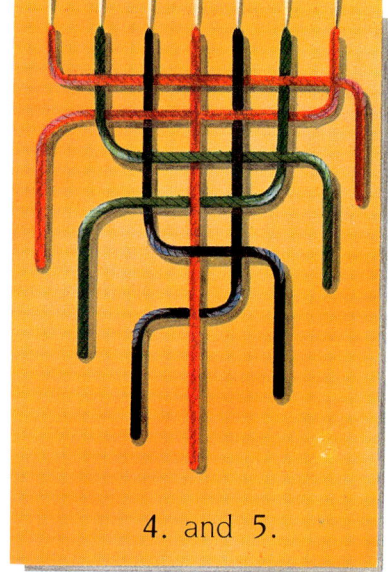
4. and 5.

CARDBOARD FISH

Try making this brightly coloured fish; then weave a whole zoo if you wish!

MATERIALS

Thin card in contrasting colours
Scissors
Pencil
Paints or crayons
Transparent sticky tape

METHOD

1. Draw and cut out a fish shape.
2. Cut a second piece of card a little smaller than the fish body (not the tail or head).
3. Lay this piece of card on the fish and draw round it.
4. Carefully cut a wavy pattern on the fish, inside the shape you have drawn.
5. Cut the smaller piece of card into strips. Number the strips on the backs to keep them in order. Starting with 1, weave these in and out of the cuts on the fish. Hold the ends in place with tape on the back of the fish.
6. Use paint or card to add fish details.

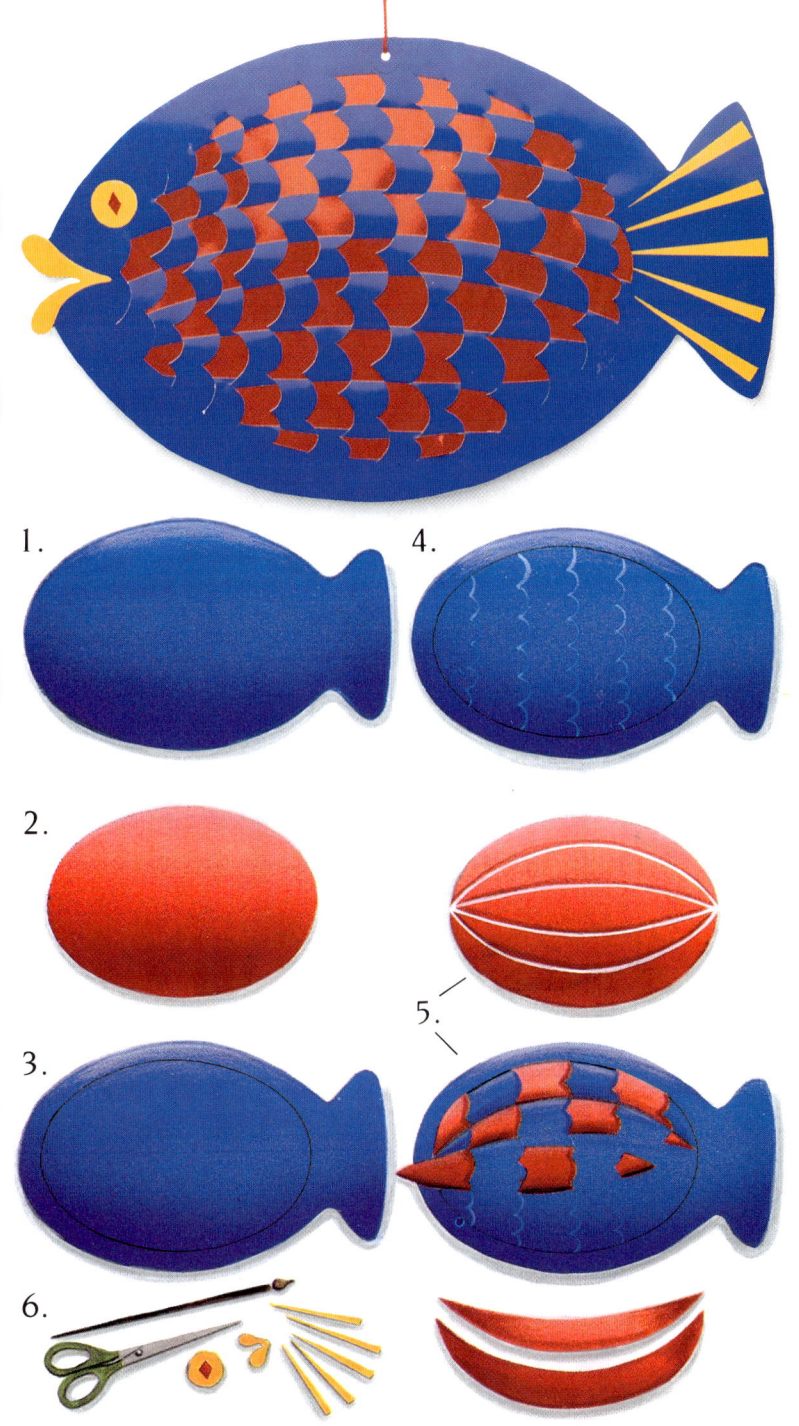

TRY MAKING
GOD'S EYES

GOD'S EYES

Mexican children call them "ojos de Dios"; you probably call them "God's eyes". Whatever you call them, they're fun to make.

MATERIALS

Brightly coloured yarn, string or raffia
Small sticks
Scissors

METHOD

1. Tie two sticks together with one end of the yarn to make a cross.

2. Start wrapping your sticks with yarn. Follow the winding directions in the diagram and hold the yarn tightly as you weave. Change colours by knotting on a new yarn. Keep going until a little before you get to the ends of the sticks. Tie off the end of the yarn.

3. Add tassels, if you like, and a loop to hang it.

Try weaving a brooch (pin) on two matchsticks, or earrings on heavy fuse wire for the cross, using fine fuse wire or threads for weaving.

You can also make God's eyes out of strips of cellophane. Hang them in your window and watch the sun-patterns on your wall.

1.

2.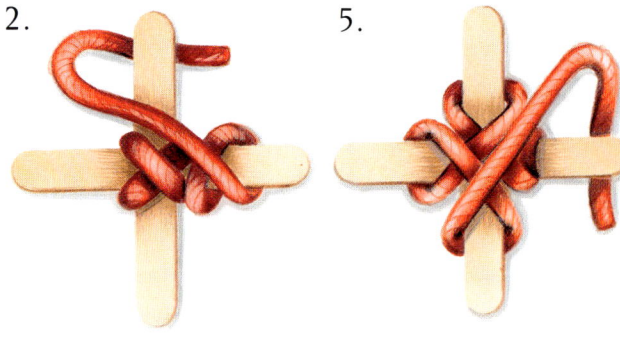

3.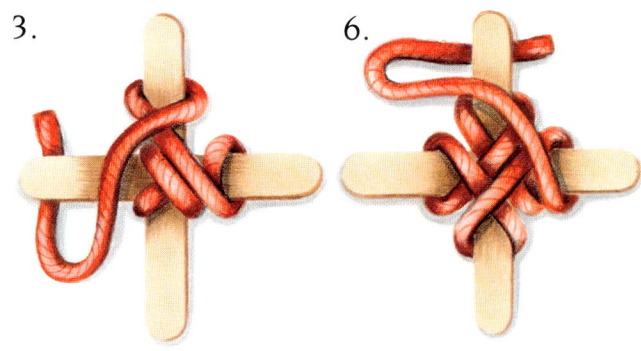

HOW TO DO
TWIG WEAVING

TWIG WEAVING

It's not necessary to use a flat loom. For something different, weave a sculpture on a twig loom.

MATERIALS

Brightly coloured yarns
Longish twigs or a branch with twigs
A tall box, carton or jar
Newspapers
For decoration: tassels, feathers, God's eyes, beads

METHOD

1. Place the twigs in the container so that they make an interesting shape. Hold in place with crumpled newspaper.

2. Start weaving! You'll find this work is something like a 3-D tangle weaving. Try to make it look interesting from all sides. Here and there, attach decorations to make your own original work of art.

WEAVING WITH
NATURAL MATERIALS

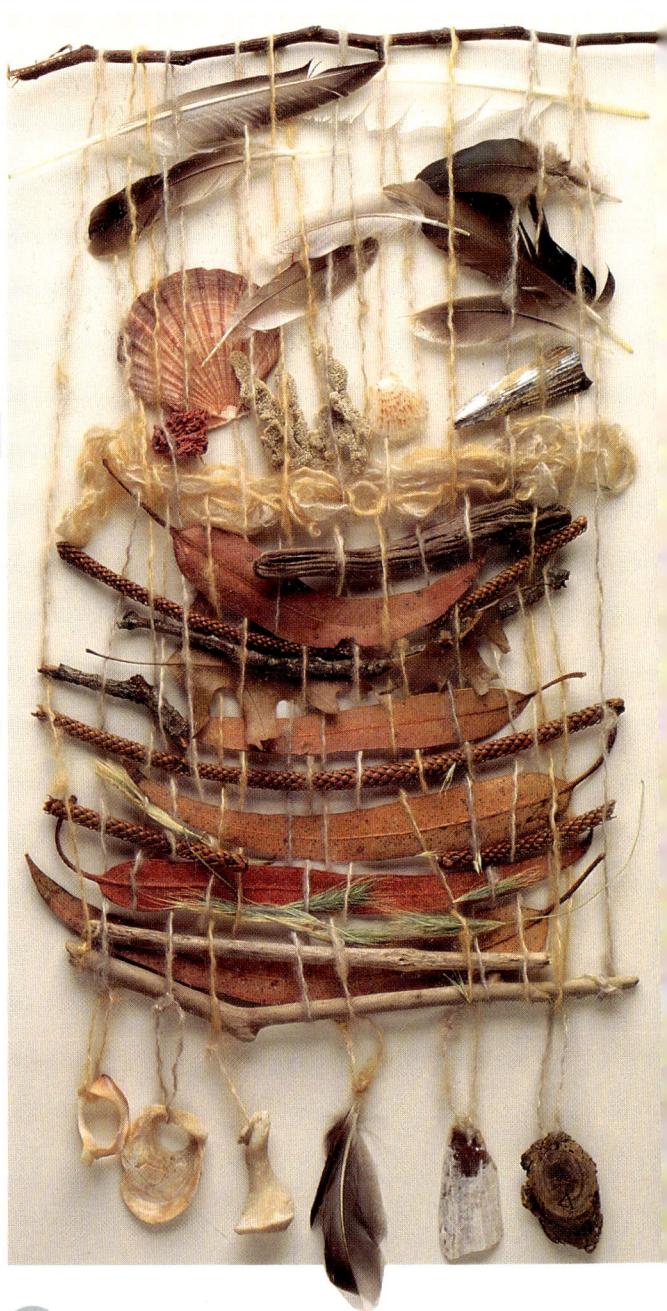

WALL HANGING

By now, you'll be ready to weave anything!

An outdoor trip will provide objects to include in your next weaving. For instance, after a walk along the beach, why not weave a hanging to display the dry seaweed, shells, driftwood, feathers and crab claws you found on the sand?

MATERIALS

Cardboard loom — see page 11
Thread or yarn
Double-sided sticky tape
2 natural rods, such as sturdy twigs, pieces of driftwood or bamboo
Other natural objects for interest

METHOD

1. String some thread on to a frame, following the first two steps for cardboard looms on page 11. Then weave in your finds as the weft.

2. Before you unhook the finished work, use double-sided tape to secure the weft articles to the warp. Gently unhook your work.

3. Slide the rods through the loops at the top and bottom. Make a decorative fringe.

FLAX BASKETS

Weave flax to make table-mats or baskets.

MATERIALS

Several strips of flax or other long leaves
1 very long strip of flax
Stapler

METHOD

1. To make a round basket, staple 4 strips (including the very long strip) together like a star. Fold the fronds up from the point where the solid bottom ends.

2. Measure and cut several long strips to fit loosely around what will become the sides of the basket. Staple the ends of each strip together to make a round.

3. Set these rounds over the 8 upright fronds, weaving as instructed for the basket on page 8. Tuck raw ends inside.

4. Staple the long strip over for a handle.

WEAVE A
BULLETIN BOARD

A BULLETIN BOARD

Make your own bulletin board and fill it with things you want to keep. It will become a personal display that you can easily change as often as you like.

MATERIALS

Sheets of coloured card — our base is 62cm by 42cm (24½in by 16½in)
Another sheet of larger card about the same size, or lengths of ribbon 1.5cm (½in)
White glue or staples

METHOD

1.   Cut strips about 2.5cm (1in) wide from the second sheet of card.

2.   Use these strips or ribbon to weave diagonal warps and wefts. Pull them firmly as you go and glue or staple the ends to the base sheet of card.

3.   Cut strips to make a frame around the border.

Now you can slot all sorts of things into your personal bulletin board.